For Sydney and Jeremy

Letters.

There's a box in my room
filled with unsent letters.
Maybe someone will read them one day
when I will no longer be there to stop them.
The letters are not addressed, or stamped.
And they're always sealed twice.
Some of them are written on the back of receipts
or napkins,
or skin.
Some are written on gold paper and tied in brown string.
I wonder if I sent them if it would change anything.
But for now I am content
with just my little box knowing how I feel
holding all my words
and keeping them safe.

Contents

The Writing

Tired of being Tired

I will bleed on paper and publish my veins.

I'll grow forests out of ink

and burn them to the ground.
for a moment.
just a moment of light.

Or a moment of warmth.

Or just to watch something burn.
I'll give you my bones,
but beg you to lay them to rest
within the creases of my books.

I'm so tired of bearing the weight
of my skin, and blood, and flesh

on these hollowed out bones

but I couldn't ask you to carry them for me.

Comet

In my head I like to connect the freckles
that are scattered across your body like stars.
I give names to the constellations I create,
imagining stories to the shapes forming on your skin.
And if I were God I'd place my world in the hollow between
your eyes
so my earth could see the Universe the way you do.
I'd kiss the fire burning your skin
until the dying stars fall
leaving a trail of light behind
like comets saying goodbye.

That Night

Head turned away Eyes closed,
half hidden.

He'd rather keep his
thoughts
to himself
than tell me he's disappointed.

Texts,
in search of human intimacy
looking
for the
validation
I crave so deeply.

I notice as he's kissing her
a look of pure sadness.

Was that sadness?
Is he lost?
I don't know.
He's not me and I'm not him
but I saw myself in him momentarily.

I want to speak
but he's asleep
and I don't think
he'd want to hear what I have to say

anyway.

The Curse Of Being a Writer

I feel everything too strongly and too deeply
Always searching for symbolism, metaphors, and similes
in places where there are none.
Every moment I'm trying to find the words to perfectly
describe how I'm feeling.
How the fog settles on my skin in the morning,
what color exactly describes the ink on my finger tips,
the taste of coffee on my tongue after a night of tossing and
turning,
trying to remember what you said when I was too drunk to
be listening.
I think I may have taken the quotation
"Either write something worth reading or do something
worth writing"
a little too seriously because
every moment I am not living I am writing
and I've been writing a lot lately.

I was in a car the other night
driving up windy roads at 2 a.m.
with my closest friends
when the driver blasted the heater
and I didn't tell him to turn it down
even though the windows were closed shut

and I felt like passing out.
I didn't tell him to stop
because I was letting myself feel
and when was the last time I let myself really feel?
Because what's the point of living if I'm always thinking
about dying?
But maybe I'm always thinking about dying
because that's the only promise I can keep.
But right now I'm letting myself feel.

I felt the sweat dripping down my back,
the McDonald's bag getting crushed beneath my feet,
the air thick with artificial salt and grease,
the song blasting on full volume as we sang loudly and out of
tune.
O.k maybe I was the only one singing out of tune but
in that moment I thought of you.
And all those nights I spent riding in the passenger seat of
your car,
loving you the only way that I could at 16
which was quietly.

I wrote you a letter and buried it in 2015.
If you start picking at that year like a scab I'm sure you would
find it
under all that healed skin.

I'm sure by now the ink has started to bleed together.
All the words I spent so long trying to make perfect
are impossible to read now.

But now your voice has been replaced with poems and stories
racing through my mind
coming up with scripted dialogue,
putting words in your mouth that you have yet to speak.
Or words you may never speak.

Because as a writer I could not just "like you" when I found you.
No liking was too simple, too soft.
No I loved you as desperately as I wrote, as feverishly as I read
as I tried to understand how someone as beautiful as you
could exist outside of a book.
Your spine held together your pages,
closed off to the world unless just the right reader sat down
and got to know you.
I don't know if I knew you well enough to understand what you were trying to say
but now that my spine has creases
and my pages dog-eared and flipped through
I think I understand a little better now.

And maybe that's why I write because no matter how many times I try
to put you down on paper you just don't seem to be satisfied with simply being a character in a story you're no longer a part of.

So I will keep writing,
and reading, and living,
and trying until I get it right.
My pen coming up with countless scenarios that will never come true
and that is my curse as a writer,
because when I write
all I can ever write about
is you.

Goodbye

There are coffee stains on my table,
three rings to be exact.
My hands are shaking from the caffeine,
but I'll take another sip,
and I never knew I could miss someone
I never had so much.

Rattlesnake

I wonder if Eve secretly liked the apple.
If when it was all over
she decided that it had been worth it.
Maybe that's why kissing you
has a sweet after taste.
I don't know why my pleasure has to be sinful,
so forget swearing on the bible.
I'll promise to always need you
with one hand wrapped around a bottle
and your hand around my throat.
I don't know how to love
without feeling like I'm chocking
on forbidden fruit.

Innocent

Little brother you have started pulling at your hair.
Clawing and picking at your beautiful red hair
and claiming that you don't mean to hurt yourself.

Little brother you have told me that if you could
you would jump off the Empire State Building,
the concrete rushing to meet you in the sky,
your soft body colliding with the ground.

Little brother you have stopped eating.

Little brother I am afraid.

Some nights when I come into your room
to kiss you goodnight
your freckles have been replaced with tears
as blue as your young eyes.

Why?

I didn't get to scream
and I didn't get to throw a wine glass
at the wall like they do in the movies.
I think that that would have been satisfying,
to hear the glass shatter,
to know that I wasn't the only thing breaking in that room.
But I didn't.
I just sat there.
I asked
who
when
where?
And no, I did not forget to ask *why?*
I didn't want to know.

And it doesn't feel fair that I never learned
to grab my anger like a bat.
To swing hard and use my voice like the weapon I know it
can be.
To use my words that I've spent years sharpening
like daggers, because I knew what I wanted to say.
I knew what would hurt you the way you hurt me.
But I didn't.
I just sat there,

and I asked you to leave.

And I think that isn't fair.
That you made me so tired I didn't even think to yell.
That I made your leaving easy
when you had made loving you so hard.

In the End

The Universe will be silent.
No wind whistling
or fires crackling
or hearts breaking.
Dusty books will hold their breaths.
Photographs will drown in the rising water,
the water is also quiet.
Afraid of taking up too much space.

Space is a cemetery. For fallen stars,
there is no light left here.
She used to take it with her morning coffee,
she liked the way the stars dissolved on her tongue.
She liked the bitter taste they left in her mouth.
The books know that about her but they can't breathe.
Do you remember me?
They ask before dissolving
since there are no more trees left to tell their story.

The Universe will be buried in rising water,
afraid of the cemetery
afraid of being forgotten.
You brought her to her knees
with all your suffering.

Can you blame her for letting the flowers die?
Can you blame her for burning down the homes
you built with her bones?
She has never been afraid of dying
but Oh God
is she terrified
of the silence.

Bright Yellow Flowers Bloom

The Rain has been making love
to the Hill outside my window
for the past few nights now.
I can hear the Earth moaning as she reaches her fingers up
to cup the Rain's face.
He kisses her neck
and wherever his fingers wander
bright yellow flowers bloom.
I have my morning coffee outside.
Rain has left
but I can still hear the evidence
of his late night presence
dripping down from the roof.
The Hill looks different this morning.
Her cheeks are flushed green
and her chest is rising up and down
rhythmically to the beating of the sun on her body.
That night I hear that Rain has come back.
He is tentatively knocking on Earth's bedroom door.
I know she has let him in when he comes pouring down.
I crawl into bed, and pull the covers up
but notice-
a yellow flower laid out on my pillow
and for a moment I feel a little less alone.

Writer

My pen stained my skin
with words I'd never write,
and the bruises forming on my fingers
matched the ones on my heart.

The Sealing

Love Story

Mom threw away your letters.
She told me over dinner,
said she couldn't bare to look at them anymore.
It has been more than five years after all.
I asked if they were still in the trash
and got up to dig them out
saying that I can hold onto them.
I've got a box that still has room for a couple more letters.
I'm good at holding onto things,
I guess it runs in the family.

She tells me she threw them out a week ago,
that there's no point holding onto them.
I tell her to stop throwing things away,
please stop throwing them away.
I don't know how to explain to her that I need to know
that they were once in love.
I don't know how a love story like theirs
can end up in the trash.
I can still see the bar in France where they first met.
I try to remember what it looked like when they were in love.
I remember waterfalls
and my dad's hand on my mother's shoulder.

I sometimes wonder if the love I have to give expired with them.
If one day my letters
will also end up
in the trash.

His

he told me that to him i was a drug,
but not a drug that destroys,
but rather heals.
that he felt this rush of euphoria whenever i touched him,
and my love coursing through his veins somehow fixed him.

i'm sure all drug addicts feel that way.

Mine

He must have thought that since sex sells
my body was a concession stand.
I had to reteach my body every night that it is a canvas
one that only I get to paint on.
I hid notes inside my collarbones
and in the nooks of my elbows
to remind myself that there are some things
that can't be taken from me.

Your Vice

Find your vice and let it kill you.
Whether it's poisoning your lungs with smoke,
buzzing your blood with caffeine,
always running late,
keeping every receipt,
or falling in love.

Find the thing that makes you human
and don't ever write about it.
Take it to your grave

so that generations to come will never know
that sometimes you cried after sex,
sometimes threw things during fights,
or hurt the people you loved most.

Take your humanity with you when you die
so that all you leave behind
are a couple receipts,
cigarette butts,
and half-brewed coffee.

I'm Sorry

Loving you
was like stealing pictures
out of someone else's wallet.

Someone was always meant to love you
so much more
than I ever could.

Runaway

There's a suitcase by my door
that never goes away.
Always packed
ready to go.
You asked me where my home was.
I said that

I don't know.

Christmas in New York

Do you remember New York?
Sleeping on that air mattress
on the floor of your grandparent's basement?
How the cold floor pressing into our backs would wake us up
because the air kept leaking out?
Do you remember sleeping in until 1 p.m. everyday?
How I felt the day was over before it even began.
On Christmas Eve my family sent me a video
of everyone sitting under the tree telling me they missed me.
I asked if we could watch Christmas movies and you said
That's not really my thing.

Do you remember listening to "Just like heaven" on that trip?
How you would sing loudly
with one hand on the steering wheel
the other on my thigh.
You knew just what trick to make me laugh,
and when I sang back I was really promising that
I would run away with you.

I dreamt that I saw you last night.
You tried to kiss me and I pushed you away.
You did run away,
like you promised.

Just not with me.

Do you remember New York?
And "Just like Heaven"?
Do you remember what it was like to kiss me?

Because I don't.
I can't even dream about it.

Starved

There are dead flowers in my room.
I keep forgetting to water them.
It is not my fault that they are so pretty
but never make any noise.

Her Drug

In the morning you don't want me anymore.
I can tell by the way you don't kiss me back.

You're drunk
you call me a drug you can't quit.
As if I'm something you need to keep secret.
A vice you can't stand.
I ask if we can talk about it.
Not now. I can't now.
But we never talk about it when you're sober.

It's been five years of this.
I don't exist at the bottom of a bottle
or at the end of a cigarette.
I exist in the morning too,
wondering what it is about the light of day that makes you
not want to look at me.
I am sorry you're so scared,
but I am not 16 anymore.
I am not a drug,

I never was.
and I am tired of being used.

Until Time do us Part

The clock in the church echoes back to me
the things left unsaid
between my mother and father.
Reminds me of the time they didn't give themselves,
the way their bird-throated voices mimicked the words
I love you
once said so genuinely
now an empty biblical promise.

Their empty palms begging for one last blood waltz,
For the blood of our children,
blood in our shame,
blood in the blessed broken wine glasses
thrown against the wall
over and over again
until the ticking of the clock
in the church stops.

Until no one is left to pray.
Until the lights are turned off
and even God has gone home.
Until the ticking of the clock echoes one last time
through the darkness
replicating their marriage.

Tick.
Tick.
Tick.
Stop.

My Poetry

He does not understand my poetry
and sometimes it makes me wonder
if it's because he doesn't really know me
or if it's because I've confined my truth to these pages.

Porn

maybe we like hair pulling
and scratching
and hitting
because sex is more about power
than love.

i've been bleeding on this bed for too long.
passion forced from my veins
through gritted teeth.

i thought i liked being slapped
until the day that he hit me and meant it.

Therapy

I can not seem to write
right now.
No, I have nothing to say.
My therapist has taken all my good ideas
right out of my head.

Fruit

He bore into me like I was unclaimed fruit.
Whether or not I wanted him to.
He smacked his lips and said
although my body looked like a freshly cut up peach
I wasn't as sweet
as he had expected me to be.
I whispered I was sorry for my bruised skin
and bitter callous flesh.

I'm just so used to being taken from.

Saint Tropez

I watched the moon cross the sky
while getting drunk on white wine.
French words
passed
through
heavy
lips
in the company of strangers,
thousands of miles from home.

Wishing I didn't have to go back.

Souvenirs

When my father went to France
he was in his early twenties.
Dressed with a half-thrown on uniform
and a carefree grin.
The world seemed to materialize
in the tiny streets of Paris.
He loved France so much in fact
that he brought home a piece of her to Texas.
A postcard wasn't good enough,
a bottle of *Merlot* tasted sweet
but would not keep him warm forever
and he did not care for knick knacks.

So he brought my mother home with him.

He liked the way wine flushed her cheeks
and how she always leaned in for *la biz* when first meeting.
Oh! How French!
His friends would exclaim
and my mother would pull back before finally realizing
that here,
in America,
we shake hands.

She was so loud.

My father could never understand what she was saying
but she said it so beautifully
that what she wanted to say
never really mattered anyway.

Naïve

sixteen was too young.
at sixteen I was still growing
still learning how to love.

now I'm just trying to learn how to love myself.

The Sun Also Sets

I realized I was in Madrid today.
Full on paella and churros
and the want for nicotine.
Walking down stone paths that twist and curve
through the ancient streets of Madrid.
The sun began to set
coloring the sky orange, and red, and pink
reflecting the colors on the fans the Spanish women used
to beat back the heat.
I came across the towering statue of Federico Lorca
and wondered if what I had to write was worth dying over.
The smell of fried sardines and cigarettes rose with the heat
mingling above the city
with the accents of the tourists
whose words didn't carry enough weight
to land anywhere in particular.
I quickly turned towards you,
almost pointed like a child to see if you had realized to.
I was met by empty space and I remembered you were not
here.

But wasn't it pretty to think so?

Safe

I think I could build a home inside of you.
A home that I wouldn't have to leave for once.

An Ode to Barney and Chocolate before Bed

When I was five
every night,
before bed,
my mom would give me hot chocolate
in my favorite green sippy cup.
She would put on Barney and Friends
and I'd think
Honestly, life can't get much better than this

I remember my first Big Disappointment.
"You're getting a little chubby," she says.
"All that milk and chocolate before bed is so bad for you.
Besides big girls don't drink from sippy cups"

I gave up Barney willingly.
Well as willingly as a child loses teeth;
I simply outgrew it.
My Dad liked to joke though,
even until I moved out,
whenever I was watching anything he'd ask
"How's Barney?"
I'd roll my eyes, as sixteen year olds do,
and he'd laugh his Dad laugh.

I get my sweet tooth from him you know.
He always has a piece of dark chocolate
and a glass of milk before bed,
even if all that chocolate and milk can't be good for him.

At least that's what my mom says.

Mon Cher

I am still jet lagged so I wake up at 5 am in the little studio apartment in Paris. My cousin never came home last night. I check my phone and notice she texted me two hours ago saying she was spending the night with a friend. I smile because that sounds like Nina all right

I get dressed and I notice it's raining outside but I didn't pack an umbrella. I wrap a scarf around my neck and make my way out of the building, into the cold air, and cross the street to enter the Boulangerie that I could smell all the way from the apartment. I order a café alongé and the best quiche I've ever had.

It's a cold and rainy day in Paris, perfect cemetery going conditions.

The *Cimtière du Père-Lachaise* is peaceful; there is no one else here besides me because of the rain. The rain is coming down more like mist now, and I appreciate the cold on my cheeks. It reminds me that I am alive. I can't help but think this place looks like a small city, with its paved roads and family crypts that look like small houses. Death does not feel so scary when it looks so familiar.

My mother always loved cemeteries, as a child I thought it was morbid but now I think I understand. I say the names I read on tombstones out loud, especially the ones that are overgrown with moss and I walk leisurely as though I were home.

I sit down on a white stone bench, and pull out my small notebook and pen. I didn't bring a pre-written letter for the lovers Héloïse and Abélard who are buried here, because for once I don't know who to address it to. I don't want to talk about the past, or my parents, or the heartbreak I just went through last month. I'm too hopeful with the grey sky above me and my feet firmly planted on this side of the ground.

Dear...

Dear...

Dear Love,

The Sending

Dear David,

You told us about it in the dressing room one night before the school play. You were laughing, your arm wrapped around the girl you were dating while the rest of us caked our face in makeup. *Yeah, I have the same one as that guy from the Fault in our Stars so that's just what I tell people.* We didn't even have a second to be concerned because you followed it with *I have an 80% survival rate so I'm gonna be ok.* And we believed you because here you were in the prime of your life just as invincible as the rest of us. But I'm not going to lie, as a writer I couldn't help but wish you hadn't compared yourself to Augustus. I couldn't help but think that that was foreshadowing.

You started missing more school until one day you stopped coming at all. But we didn't worry because we knew you were coming back. I mean you had a play to direct, a mock trial team to lead, colleges to apply to. We didn't worry when months went by. We didn't even worry when you finally came to visit you were in a wheel chair and all your hair was gone. You just laughed and joked about what kind of cane you should get. We didn't worry, except that we did. But you always made it seem so impossible that there could be any other outcome other than you being ok.

Of course, isn't that how it always goes?

David,
the day of your funeral
was one of the hottest days I remember.
It felt insensitive of the Universe
to let the sun shine so brightly
that November day.
That week in school
we wrote your name on the dressing room wall
and decorated your locker with White Roses.

I thought about you the other day, randomly while I was at the beach. It's almost been four years since you passed away and sometimes I still check your Instagram. I don't know why. I've been trying to write to you all this time but I just didn't know how. I still don't know how. I don't know what to say other than you are missed.

I just needed to send you this letter. I think it's important.

From the Perspective on a Hamster Wheel

I realized the other day
that to my hamster,
I am God.
When I enter the room
her world shakes.
The sun rises and sets
when I decided to flip the light switch.
Her reality is the one that I created.
I don't know what to do with my newfound status as a deity.
She is, after all, only a hamster.
I wonder if this is how our God feels
(Whoever or whatever that may be).
If when He looks at us
He ever pities us for how little space we take up in the
Universe.

Maybe God is just a kid,
who bought us at the flea market when He read on our box
"Just add water and watch life grow!"
I imagine He hung us on His ceiling,
held up by string
dangling near marbled shaped planets
and glow in the dark stars.
I don't think God was ready to be worshipped.

He must have been busy with school projects,
and cleaning his room,
and first crushes.
I'm sure that as we grew,
God did too.

Maybe God fell in love,
and really,
who can blame a love struck teenager
for forgetting about us?
But sometimes when they sit alone in His room together,
He turns off all the lights and whispers to her.
"There's Saturn! And that's Venus.
I can give you one of them to take home with you if you'd
like"
He tells her about how His mother helped Him stick
all those glow in the dark stars on His ceiling when He was
little.
"Which one is that?" She asks one night.
"That's Earth."
"How silly," she giggles. "It looks like it's made of mostly
water."
He blushes softly,
"I may have read the instructions wrong and added too
much."
This makes her love Him even more.

And so God, I don't know if I can forgive you.
For the war, and the pain, and the hatred.
But I think I can understand
that it may have been too much responsibility,
and that we were originally just a science experiment.
And I understand what it feels like to be in love.
I used to trace a boy's tattoos like they were my stars
and gave him parts of me to take home with him like they were my planets
when I had nothing else to give.
I didn't know how to fix us either
and I am only God to a hamster.

Home

My mother's accent
will always feel more like home
than any four walls
ever could.

How to Stop Saying "I'm Sorry"

Recognize that you are saying it.
So often that the sound of it is more familiar
to you than your own name.
Recognize that you have started walking into rooms
with your back curving into a question mark
for a question you haven't even asked yet.
How that question is *am I worth being here?*

Flip back through childhood journals
and old photo albums.
See how much space you used to take up with your little
body.
Remember how loud you used to be.
When another kid pushed you
you pushed them right back.

Remember the first time a boy snapped
the strap of your training bra.
This was the first attack on your body,
you were told he only did it because he probably liked you.
This was how you were taught to apologize
for the way your body was becoming "too woman".

Recognize that you are saying it.

Instead of *move*
Instead of *no*
Instead of *stop*
Remember that your words
are the only weapon you have ever known.

Do not limit your arsenal to an apology.

11/20/2018

I guess I should say thank you
for the way that you left.
It made me realize
that I never could have truly loved
somebody as selfish as that.

The Breakup

you said you didn't want me anymore.
you said "I have always thought of you as fire."
i used to take that as a compliment,
i never knew you thought that
because you were getting ready to run.

i once said that i thought
i could build a home inside you.
one I wouldn't have to leave
for once.
while i was unpacking my suitcase
in the space between your neck and shoulders,
behind your knees,
on your chest,
you were looking for the fire exit.

but then again I wouldn't want to let a wild fire
into my home either.
being from california
i've seen the damage
fire can cause.

someone once told you
"You can't handle a girl like her."

offended i said “I don’t need to be handled.”
but i just wish someone would stay
long enough to feel my warmth.
to see my light
and not the charred trees i’ve left behind.

to see that all i’ve ever wanted
was a place to call home.
and i thought that could be you.

Keep the Lights On

So
I wore the lingerie that I had bought
with you in mind
for him
last night.

I figured I shouldn't let it go to waste.

I figured he would like it
and
it was getting depressing
just looking at it in my drawer.

I try not to think about it,
I guess it's not that weird since he's already
touched me,
and
kissed me,
not exactly
the way you
used to
but in all the same places.

It's like the same song but with different lyrics

and I'm still learning all the words.

I don't know why I'm telling you this.
I guess it's because I was excited to wear it for you
and when you came home form
work
I asked you if you
liked it and you
said
Sure

Then you turned off the lights.

I was just thinking about it.

I was thinking about how he called me
beautiful.

I was thinking about how he didn't turn
off the lights.

Jonathan's Bar

If I focus hard enough
I can almost see my parents
meeting for the first time.
The American
and the French woman
falling in love.
I have heard this story so many times
I can watch it unfold in front of me.

He whispers to his friend,
Tell her she is the most beautiful woman I have ever seen.
She blushes and smiles back.
They laugh for the rest of the night
taking sips from their beers
just as I am right now.
They are so unaware that 20 years from now
their daughter will return to the scene of the crime.
I am so happy all this bar has ever known of them
is love

What's Left Unsaid

I'm trying to spend more time with my little sister
so we're here
at the Little Italy farmer's market
even though we both have no money.
I ask her about school and remember that's a touchy subject,
but before long we're laughing
as we pass stands of fresh fruit
and pots of organic honey.

We walk by a stand that's selling crêpes
for 15 dollars a pop and both scoff.
We were both raised on Nutella and caramelized bananas
cracking eggs in bowls
mixing flour, milk, and sugar
before we were even tall enough to reach the kitchen table.
I could make that for a dollar
I want to mention Mom
but I don't know when the two of them last spoke.

We buy a Panini to share and sit at the base of a fountain,
it's a beautiful sunny day
and I say we should make this a tradition
with all the best intentions.
She nods,

the cheese spilling out from her half of the sandwich
as she takes a bite
and suddenly I remember her as a 6 year old girl.
Her blonde hair pulled back in pigtails
her two front teeth missing and snails covering her hand
as we played in the backyard.
Back before everything got so messed up.

Snails are still her favorite insect to this day
(even though they're not *actually* insects)
and so her nickname for me always makes me smile.

We get up and suddenly she walks over to a flower stand
and buys me a bouquet of red flowers.
I tell her to keep her money
but she hands them to me anyway.
I take out my wallet and buy her yellow flowers
and in this moment I'm saying sorry.
Sorry for that horrible fight
back when I hated her for taking up so much space
back when I was angry and I didn't understand
why she couldn't get out of bed.
When I yelled at her:

You're the reason Mom and Dad got divorced!

I want her to know that I know that's not true
and I regret it everyday.
That I know this day doesn't make up for it but I'm trying.
She smiles,
takes the flowers and says

Thanks Snail.

101 Voicemails

There are 101 voicemails on my phone.
They are all from my mother.
That is 101 times I didn't answer her call.
Maybe I was sleeping,
or in class.
Maybe I was at the movies
or work
or I simply didn't want to talk.
101 times I could have said
I love you.
Sometimes I like to listen to them all at once.
I miss you
Let me know how you're doing
Call me back
Je t'aime
I never delete them.

I am almost twenty
but the other day
as we were crossing the street
my mother reached down and grabbed my hand.
I have been crossing the street alone
for almost ten years.
I almost told her this

but then I let her lead me.
It was nice to not worry about the cars for once.
I realized that I haven't called out for my Maman in 30 years.
One day you won't be able to either.
She laughs as if she's teasing.
I hold her hand a little tighter.
Je t'aime Maman.
I love you too.

The Ridge

IV.

Would you like a cigarette?

I shake my head, no.
You flick your lighter open and watch me walk to my car.
I hear you call out after me,

That poem you wrote still makes me cry.
You know, the one about Madrid.

Without looking up I shout back,

I hope it makes you cry forever.

II.

This is my favorite place in the world.
It's late, around 2 a.m.
and we're sitting at the edge of The Ridge
overlooking the I-five.
I ask you where you think all those cars are going.
He's going home to his girlfriend,
she'll probably be mad because his shift ended two hours ago.

I laugh
That car right there is full of teenagers driving home from a concert in LA.
Everyone is asleep except for the driver.
He's looking at the girl in the passenger seat,
he can't stop thinking about how beautiful she looks.
What about that car right there?
Oh they're not going anywhere.
They're just driving.

III.

Today is graduation.
We came straight here after the ceremony
because where else would we go?
I'm still wearing my graduation robe
I stand on the wooden fence and throw my arms up.
WE DID IT. WE FUCKING DID IT. Oh my God was the world always this big?
I climb down and you're looking at me funny.
I ask you what's wrong. You pause and say
I love you.
I punch your shoulder and laugh.
I love you too, dork.
No. No, I love *you.*

I.

I've only known you for a few months,
but I already can't imagine my life without you.
You've got a place to show me.
You guys call it The Ridge.

IV.

I'm waiting for you. I haven't seen you in two weeks.
I missed you but when you walk over and try to hug me
I shake my head, no.
You slowly drop your arms.
I don't want to do this here,
this is where we fell in love.
It's just a little too poetic,
even for me.
I say *It feels like you don't even want to be with me anymore.*
You say
I don't think I do.

IV.

You ask me if I'd like a cigarette.

IV.

I shake my head, no.

IV.

You watch me walk to my car

IV.

You watch me drive away

IV.

I only start to cry when I can no longer see you in the rearview mirror

IV.

I wonder why you won't fight for us

IV.

V.

I'm here,
alone.
Of course it feels different,
but I'm still sad it feels different.
The view is the same.
The cars are still driving,
they are always going to be driving
even when no one is here to assign them a backstory.
It feels like this place is the setting to an old story.
Like I've flipped back the pages of my book to reread this part of my life
only to find that the characters aren't here anymore.
That this place isn't for me anymore.

And it isn't.
But that's ok,
because the world has always been
so much bigger than this,
anyway.

Taking it Back

when a song comes on that reminds me of you i don't skip it anymore/ i say to myself *this is mine. this reminds me of me. this song belongs to me. i'm making new memories* / and it works/ for a second/ it's hard to listen to the songs we listened to/ on our way to LA that one summer/ but i still do/ i try not to remember the observatory/ the hole in the wall book shop where i bought my favorite poetry book/ how i read "Le Petit Prince" in french to you and you said that if i let you love me you would do it right/ i listened to those songs the whole time i was in france/ granted because they reminded me of you/ but now i'm trying to replace you with something/ beautiful/ with the beaches with bright blue water/ the nights that i got drunk on cheap wine with my cousin/with the dancing/ i remember the boy who tried to kiss me but i told him no because i was already in love/ now i think about how i let the boys and girls who want to kiss me/ kiss me. i put extra creamer in my coffee because you used to say coffee was only good black/ i think, *fuck you* with every sugar packet/ i roll my windows down/ and let the wind mess up my hair/ i remember that you stopped playing our songs a while ago/ i realize all of this was always mine and you were just a character/ passing through/ i realize how much harder it will be for you/ to forget me.

Realization

I've got flowers in my hair
and sinning on my mind
and I'm so sorry mom
but I just don't give a damn
because she's spring in autumn
and moonlight on my skin.

Red

The woman with red hair,
puts on a red dress,
applies red lipstick to her lips,
and throws her red purse over her shoulder.
She gets into her red car
and drives somewhere beautiful.
When asked "Why the color red?"
She replies

Because it's loud,
and they tried to shut me up.

Breathe

Let your poetry breathe.
Let her dress down
no heels or bras or skin tight skirts.
She'll dance between the lines of your paper
skipping over punctuation, dictionary picked words and
forced rhymes.
Some days your poetry will forget how to dance.
Do not worry.
Let her rest nestled in the corner of a page dreaming of
metaphors and similes.
Remember even muses need to sleep.
Let her unpack her heavy suitcase in the hollows of your
bones
replacing marrow with paper, pens, and soul.

Never tell her that her words aren't good enough because
they don't follow
a pattern,
a rule set,
a robotic flow of rhyming words.
She'll get too nervous to tell you
how she really feels
holding back all the things you need to hear.

Let your poetry breathe
Let her write
Let her live.
When she is ready she will be imperfect, raw, and real.
The curves of her body waltzing with your words,
breathing them to life.
And maybe if you're lucky she will kiss you softly.
She will hold you against her breast and you will hear her
heart beating
ink pumping through her veins
pumping, pumping, pumping.

And when your hand collapses on your page
like a lover
too exhausted to stay awake
remember
that you too
need to let yourself
breathe.

Kind of Day

It's a sunburnt lips,
sleepy sun kissed
kind of day.
Summer day, going down to the beach
kind of day.
Finally said goodbye last night,
starting to feel ok again
kind of day.
Paddle board hitting your hip,
gonna leave a bruise but you don't care
kind of day.
Knowing that today you are twenty
and you still have so many more mistakes to make.
Feeling that familiar ache in your chest
but it hurts a little less than what you're used to.
Thinking this is an echo of a greater heartbreak,
as you feel the sun on your face
and the cold water lapping at your feet.
It's a new beginning kind of day.
Go home and wash the sand off.
Feel the warm water on your sunburnt shoulders.
Remember that you are alive.
Fall asleep in the hammock outside.
We're in no rush, we've got no where to be.

Dad

There's a video of me as a baby
barely three months old,
sleeping, bundled up in white blankets
and clean clothes.
My father still has all his hair
and he doesn't sounds as tired.
He pats my head and laughs my name
I begin to stir and gurgle.
"Oh no. Oh no don't cry! It's your dad."
The title is still so new to him,
a suit that doesn't yet quite fit.
Eighteen years have passed since then
and my father has his bearings.
He's had this gig three times by now
and he thinks he knows what he 's doing.
"I've tried to do my best by you,
I'm sorry if I've failed.
I wish I knew back then
all the things that I do now.
I could have saved you a bit of heartache
saved your siblings from my mistakes."
I've seen my father cry by now
it reminds me that he's human.
I feel comforted to know

that he was once like me.
A little lost,
with a whole life to lead.
"You've made a few mistakes," I say.
"But that's to be expected.
You've always done your best by me.
You've always been my dad."

Bessie the Grand Jeep Cherokee

Her favorite color is red
so I guess you could say
we were meant for each other.

We were both 16 when we first met.
I sat patiently in her driveway,
waiting for her to come home from work,
with a big red bow on top of me-
you know just like in the movies!
No one has ever been so excited to see me as her.
Her little sister and brother had left a card on my driver seat,
it had a big dinosaur on the front
and they wrote inside,
"You're getting so old!"
she put it in my glove compartment and it's been there ever since.

She listens to a lot of musicals.
Recently a lot of true crime podcasts.
It makes her drive faster at night
when we're coming home from work.
There's been a lot of important people
that have sat in my passenger seat.
Some I haven't seen in a few years.

It makes me sad because she always did sing louder
when they were here.
Sometimes we pass by the house of one of those girls,
one of those important girls
that I haven't seen for a while.
She'd never admit it but I notice how we slow down.
How she looks out the window as we pass by.

She cries sometimes.
She screamed really loud
once and her hands were shaking
as she tried to grip my wheel.
I got her home safe though
as I always do.
And I haven't heard that scream since.

I love the beach days.
When she smells like sunscreen and she rolls my windows down.
She gets back in covered in sand but that's ok.
We drive home as the sun is setting
and I know today was a Good Day.
I've been here for a lot.
A lot of late night talks with my seat pushed back.
A few first kisses where we'd drive home blushing.
I helped her move when she was 18

and then again a year later.
Alone the second time,
except for me.

I see the way she looks at the Highway,
how she presses on the gas a little harder
causing me to stutter.
She always pats my dash and says
"Shhh, I'm sorry baby."

She knows I'm getting older,
but I can still keep up with her adventures.

The Cookie to the Flower Vase

After Sarah Kay's The Toothbrush to the Bicycle Tire

I have always thought that I crumble too quickly.
That I am too easily softened
with sweet milky words
spoken by those who feel like they can't handle me
without a chaser.

You tell me that you don't mind
being called *practical* instead of beautiful.
I'm used to the leaving you say.
To the changing colors and dying promises.
Even if I am overlooked at least I always stay.

I have never seen
more beautiful curves
on anyone else.
I tell you I am worried
I will disappear like sugar on your tongue
when we first kiss.
That I'm worried I've been left
on the kitchen counter for too long
and that maybe my love has gone stale.

You say that we are from different worlds,
but for once it feels nice to be noticed.
I think I could spend a few hours
counting your chocolate chip freckles
while you tell me about your day.
I am good at holding things together
and I promise I will not let you crumble away.

When you Receive the Letter

She asks me if she will be in my book.
I don't know what to answer so in a way I don't.
I still remember how we would exchange letters in class.
I tell her that it's funny,
I still have those in a box somewhere.
Notes she gave me before opening night,
letters we passed back and forth in Geometry,
all the letters she wrote me when she went away to college.
I never thought much of it,
but here she is texting me three years after high school
and I think I realize for the firs time
that she never missed a week.
Always wrote back to me immediately
even when I sometimes forgot.
I just have something I need to tell you.
I ask, why now?
Because sometime things in life are meant to be said
and I needed you to know.
I was so caught up in writing letters that I never sent
that I never noticed someone else
had been writing some for me.
I'm glad I held onto them.
Even though I didn't know what they meant.

The Mountains

And I think
I’m not as lonely
as I thought I would be.
Because through all the noise
and lost time
I forgot to be with myself.
And here I am
confronted
face to face
with who I am
and who I want to be

Dear Love,

You have tried to make me fear you,
and I can't blame you for that.
A lot of people have said some pretty horrible things about you.
Like how you aren't real, or all you cause is heartache.
I get it.
I understand pushing people away.
But I'm here to tell you I'm not afraid anymore.
I know that our relationship needs work
but I'm here and I'm willing.
I've loved so many people,
not all have stayed.
I don't blame you for that either.
I appreciate that you're always here even when it hurts.
You are coffee
and kissing under the blankets when it's raining outside.
You are poetry,
my little sister's art,
saying *I'm sorry*,
and home.

But you are also heartbreak,
and bed ridden mornings,
the apology I have nightmares about,

torn up photographs,
and unsent letters.

You are not always beautiful but neither am I.

I can appreciate you for all that you are,
even when you must leave.
I know you are making way for bigger and better things.

Dear Love,

I think I am ready
to let you
love me back

Acknowledgment Letters

Dear Mom and Dad,
Thank you for always supporting my passions and me. Thank you for every play, Improv show, and open mic you've attended. You have always nurtured the artist in me, both in different ways. Thank you Dad for always being in the audience and encouraging my love of reading by giving me a new book every time I see you. Mom, thank you for telling me to follow my heart and for asking for a poem every mother's day, birthday, or holiday. Thank you both for believing in me.

Dear Sydney and JJ,
You make me so proud to be your big sister. You are both incredible artists and I cannot wait to see how you use your talent to change the world. Sydney, thank you for our patio talks and being one of my greatest supporters. Your belief in me gave me the courage to write this book. JJ you inspire me every day with your comics, drawings, movie trailers, raps, and skits. I love you both so much.

Dear Mads,
You were the first one to hold the very primitive manuscript of *Unsent Letters* three years ago when it was still being called *A Collection.* I am so grateful to have a friend like you in my life who believed in me back when I thought it would be

impossible to ever show the world my work. Thank you for asking to read my poetry on your 18th birthday that night on the beach, it meant the world to me then and it means the world to me now.

Dear Kathleen and Brenna,
You ladies are my sunshine and my cup of tea. I cannot put into words how much I appreciate your friendship. Kathleen, "Truth Hurts" will always be our anthem when we make our way to the San Diego Poetry Slam. I am in awe of your writing journey, you are such an incredible poet and I am so proud to see how far you've come in such little time. Brenna, knowing that you have a terrible fear of public speaking and seeing you perform your first poem at Glassless Minds was an empowering experience and it helps me to remember that whenever I have fears about sharing my work. Thank you both for your endless support.

Dear Andrew,
Thank you for the camping trips, Mimosa Sundays, bekkis, and your help titling a few of the poems in this book. I am so grateful that I have you in my life you have no idea. Thank you for campfires and dancing under the stars, the world is just a little more beautiful when I get to explore it with you.

Dear Christian,
I can say without a doubt this book would not exist without you. Meeting you and talking to you about your book *What it Means to Feel Human* was the first time I ever considered that it would be possible to publish *Unsent Letters.* Thank you for always being down to give me feedback on a poem. You and I were meant to be friends, even the Tarot cards agree.

Dear Ms. Cullen,
Thank you for being one of the only people in my life to tell me to stop saying "I'm sorry" all the time. I never considered myself a writer until I took your class sophomore year of high school and you convinced me to submit to a short story contest. You are a wonderful teacher and mentor.

Dear Camp Bravo,
Thank you for changing my life. I am the person and creator I am today because of the magic you create up the Mountain. Thank you for poetry night, it is an experience I will remember for the rest of my life. From the bottom of my heart thank you so much for everything you do and for letting me be a part of that magic. I have so much love for my Bravo family.

Dear Sabrina Benaim, Clementine von Radics, and the entire Slumber Party Retreat,
Getting to experience and learn from such incredibly talented people helped me to grow not only as a writer but also as a person. Thank you Sabrina for your wonderful words on the back of this book. I feel so lucky to have met all of you and thank you for the constant support, feedback, and love.

To everyone who has broken my heart or whose heart I have broken,
En somme si j'ai compris
Sans amour dans las vie
Sans ses joies ses chagrins
On a vécu pour rien.
-Édith Piaf
Thank you for the joys and heartache.

And finally: Dear reader,
Thank you for taking the time to listen to what I have to say. I don't know if I believe in souls, but if they exist, I'd like to let you know that you are holding mine. I am so grateful to you. If you have a letter written somewhere I hope that maybe you send it. Thank you, thank you, and thank you.

Sincerely,
Margaux

Made in the USA
Middletown, DE
07 November 2019